MY KVETCH

TRUE CONFESSIONS OF A
DEMOCRAT POLITICIAN

Steven L. Baird

Printed in the United States of America

First Printing, 2018

ISBN 978-7328942-1-1

DEDICATION

To Beelzebub:

You are an originalist; the primogeniture of anarchy which is truly the purest form of man's expression on his own annihilation. You are the snake in our garden offering apples to all the sheep in the world. To my fellow anarchists... baa, baa, baa

An ode to that crazy Nazi bastard:

You stole the title of my book nearly 100 years ago. That is why I had to go with my second choice "My Kvetch". I'm sure the Jewish side of your family would be proud.

To my fellow Snowflakes:

We are all unique in character, form and function. Blow on the winds and let your individuality show the world that we can all live together in peace and harmony where there are no borders, no governments, just the base love of mankind to light our way to our destiny. Only remember, individuality will only get us so far. To make a real difference in the world, we must be slammed together, tightly molded into an organism of someone else's desire. Only then can we be weaponized on the battlefield of life. No single snowflake has ever harmed a soul, but pack enough snow together and we can dent your head. Question is, who's hands fashioned us together?

FORWARD

If you believe that this book is written for you, then congratulations, I got your money and I get to entertain you as well. There is so much going on in our country today and so many different perspectives of those goings on that I decided to write the Rosetta Stone for those who do not speak "progressive."

Full disclosure; I'm a card-carrying Democrat politician who's written the truth about a myriad of headline subjects in a unique but informative fashion. The journey on which you are about to embark is written as if I were being grilled on 60 Minutes or on a panel debate against my most worthy political opponents. My responses to the chapter heading "questions" are exactly as I would answer in either of these venues.

What you are about to read may not be the truth, but it is the truth as I understand my world today. So Alice, care to join me down the rabbit hole?

Contents

On Growing Up

I was born in Oakland, California for the strict purpose of being able to point out an affinity to a population with which I have nothing in common. My journey toward elitist nihilism had begun.

Hatched by two lower lower class (white trash) parents, I endured the nightmarish existence of growing up in different apartment complexes in sketchy neighborhoods just to survive. We ate things you wouldn't know were actually sold as food such as chicken livers and hearts (in bonus packs), mussels (we had to go to Half Moon Bay to harvest this free food) and other delicacies that kept our family lean and mean.

I had the great privilege of attending eight different schools K-12 which taught me how to be self-reliant and a devout introvert, wall flower, hazing target who was blessed with the genetic predisposition of being vertically challenged and nearsighted. This entropy into one's self created an intellectual bulwark that was being forged to join the world's elite minds who know what's best for all of us.

College for me was a means to an end. Although part Mexican, I was blue eyed and blond haired so I could not tap into those funding sources that could afford me an extended stay in the shrine of academia. I had to get through as fast as I could by tricking my advisors into letting me take way too many courses over too little time. My fellow dorm rats said it could not be done: getting through the College of Engineering in four years. I did it in three and a half without completely destroying my GPA or drinking my brain cells into oblivion. I left intact, proving my superior talents and intellect are worthy participants on the stage set only for the few, the egotistical, the elites.

Upon graduation, I immediately joined corporate America as a programmer/ analyst. My instincts to hitch my wagon to a top tier manufacturing firm in the electronic memory sector was only thwarted by an evil Japanese plot to dump product on the market far below cost to eliminate the American competition. The company had just tripled their manufacturing floor space and was working three shifts. Layoffs ensued and I was out on my ass in ten weeks. When being let go, I was informed that it was not my talent, energy or output that made me the department's target for the layoff, it was that I was young and single and the other guy was moved 1,400 miles with his wife and kids. Now, would that be fair to keep me?

I returned home to California and took the first gig I could get before I ran out of money; I worked for the large military industrial complex. I worked for the man. I was an American that built shit that could erase fourteen points of civilization in one launch. The power was consuming and the money wasn't bad. Little did I know that I had a penchant for picking losers. In less than six years, the company restructured and my division came under the management of another and we were systematically laid off regardless of race, creed, color or gender. We just worked for the wrong fucking side of the house. My badge was blue, not green ergo I was marked for termination. The great technology migration from my former employer had begun. I landed on my feet in a government position where I've sat secure ever since.

On Perspective

I was raised in a time of war where my parents were the flower children of the age. To my suspected horror, I'm sure I was made to run naked through the park. They were McGovern Democrats who hated the war and believed there was another way through peace and love. I had great role models. I just didn't get a clue until now.

On Politics

It takes many years to develop the keen sense of irony that a journey of a thousand miles can still end very badly. Just ask salmon who unwittingly jump into the mouth of a grizzly bear after that long upstream battle. The same can be said for any budding politician who does not run as a Democrat in California. I know I have what it takes to engineer the lives of my fellow people (citizens is a bit too exclusive) for the betterment of the planet. The goal is to serve one's self and to have a seat at that glorious table set only for the most worthy; those of us devoid of a single shred of moral fiber or conscience. Power is the goal and I want a taste. No, I want to gorge myself on the ambrosia of complete and utter control over mankind.

But where to begin. As you can see from earlier pages, I'm in the habit of picking the wrong horse; a divining rod for future failures. To wit, I joined the Republican Party and ran for state Senate in a very conservative district in Northern California.

What an unmitigated disaster that was. I wasn't running against the left, I was running against the entrenched right and a man who'd already read the rules and set up the chess board. I didn't have a chance in hell and he knew it. He was even so successful at the game that he has his wife trailing behind him to pick up his legislative seats as he ascends to the next level of his political career. Instead of running as his opponent, I should have volunteered to be one of his aids so I could learn the mastery of the game like so many of those sycophants with which he surrounds himself to do his every bidding. Hell, in performing the illusion of representing one million people, these aids actually have some assemblance of real power as no one person can adequately respond to so many constituents.

Yoda, I apologize for not coming into the hollow tree and learning directly from your tutelage. In taking the path of the outsider, I've learned less, gained little; the experience has been the ultimate instructor. I am ready. From birth, I fought my path. No longer. Today is the day I leave principles behind and offer myself upon the altar of power. Today I embrace all I can become. Today, I am a Democrat.

On Switching Sides

Not sure who coined the phrase, but here it is apropos; "the ends justify the means." If one is willing to give up one's conscience and put his soul up for sale to reach the promised land of power, then so be it. Actually, it is somewhat liberating to give up the shackles of principles. Is this not the height of progressiveness? The ability to adapt to any situation in order to wind up on top must be a characteristic to applaud. If you think there are actually two sides, then you're horribly misinformed. Both sides know that there is only one team to be on, team ME! It does not matter at all which color you wear onto the field as long as you can set yourself up for the win.

On Trump

Yes, we lost. We put up an untrustworthy megalomaniac who had it in the bag. A candidate who could not lower herself to kiss one baby or feign a human countenance for just a few weeks in order to further the cause.

Instead, we must now go on the offensive and create a climate of chaos and anarchy to drown out the message of a man who's done nothing but attempt to deliver on every promise he made during his campaign. We cannot abide this situation. We must use every measure possible to ensure we get back on track towards the utopian dream of non-government by the few. Why should we let this Twitter-nut have four years of our lives? The previous eight years were unobstructed bliss where the cowards of the Republican Party bowed to our every whim and fancy. It was almost a miracle that they finally found the spine to block our Supreme Court nominee in the closing months of his highness' reign.

Think of all the wonders we created during our turn at the helm. We equalized the US presence around the globe by first apologizing for our past sins then we eviscerated our military but still managed to pay for the defense of other nations including our sworn enemies. We ignored the sage advice of Thomas Jefferson and buried our nation in debt by doubling our deficit to $20 trillion dollars. This all pales in comparison to our Affordable Health Care Act which provides nearly worthless insurance to the poor and unemployed at the expense of the working middle class who suffered mightily from the lies and misrepresentations delivered through that winning smile. How we could have lost this election to that political neophyte is astounding.

On Women's Reproductive Rights

This one is easy. No one person should be able to tell another what to do with one's own body. We must abide by the constitution and clearly protect our rights as individuals.

The byproduct of Roe has incalculable value. As my hero Margaret Sanger espoused, we have the ability to cull the herd of the poor and the ignorant. The huge benefit of this program is nipping the financial burden in the bud (I mean umbilical cord). Instead of over populating our country with the lower end of the spectrum (read that as non-whites), we can legally snuff out that tiny heartbeat BEFORE it winds up on the public dole (eugenics). Raising the unwanted would cost society countless tens of millions of dollars and that is before we have to incarcerate the little bastards. The only downside to this nearly perfect construct is we are inadvertently killing our future electoral base; those dependent on the government who will vote for us in perpetuity.

The true upside of this program is if we can convince the sheeple to kill their unborn children in utero, then we can eliminate God from our lives and place man upon the throne.

On Universal Health Care

"You can keep you doctor and your health plan." Nuff said. We hired the best snake oil salesman not only once, but twice. Since the late 1800's, we've developed a blueprint to take over not just our country but the world at large.

Who can argue that health care for all is the true measure of compassionate and moral people. In practice, it is a right! Who wants to see children starving in the streets, suffering from untold maladies (at least those who managed to escape the vagi-vacuum in our other aforementioned program)? You'd have to be heartless not to be willing to give more than you have to those trapped in poverty for the good of mankind. The government was specifically created to support the "General Welfare" of those who have less and clearly deserve more.

ACA fits this paradigm to a tee. More for the have nots at the expense of the middle where it doesn't affect the one- percenters who actually believe this is a good idea. A program man-made for the disruptive benefit of all.

In actuality, the full force of ACA has not come to fruition. We've been receiving additional "junk" tax forms and we are clueless as to what they are for. When we regain power (and we always do), we'll be able to lower the threshold on what counts as a Cadillac health plan in order to raise additional taxes to redistribute to our supporters and our base.

ACA is a gift that will keep on giving for decades to come. If the neocons try to unwind the nightmare we've created, we will reap the benefit. We will be able to slingshot back to power sooner rather than later when the pyramid scheme collapses under their watch. When we authored legislation that brought about this transformative economic destruction, we truly altered the reality of hope and change. Comrade Marx is smiling down upon us.

On Gun Rights and the 2nd Amendment

This is something about which I am truly passionate. The dirty little secret is that the 2nd Amendment was shoehorned into the Constitution for one reason only. To blow our fucking brains out - the oligarchic pricks running the government outside the will of the people. This obviously cannot be tolerated and we must use all our power to disarm the disaffected masses before they catch on.

People are not smart enough to arm themselves with the modern assault weaponry of mass destruction that is available today. When it took 20-40 seconds to reload a musket, it gave the operator time to think about what they were actually doing. If we can get to the point where we make the operator take one minute per shot, America will be a much safer place.

The elephant in the room is the necessity of disarming the public at large. See, an armed and informed public can rise up against a tyrannical government where an unarmed populous is defenseless. How else would we be able to force all the bullshit we shovel their way and have them meekly accept it as gospel? Hitler, Stalin, Mao; damn, we're in some pretty impressive company.

Thankfully, we can rush in anytime our government clearly breaks down and lets some known mentally deranged individual kill a bunch of people at a school. We'll march out all the kiddies and have them protest their leaders to get them to remove the weapons of mass annihilation from the public domain. We'll be only happy to oblige. An unarmed society is a very compliant one. Just ask the aforementioned gentlemen: Mao, Hitler, Stalin, in case you need reminding.

After the sheep accept the licensing of ammunition sales and break gun loading statues, we'll make it a felony to create a noise above 130 decibels with the use of a hand held or shoulder braced device. That should kill the gun argument forever.

Of course, I plan to join the elite that has already exempted itself from the myriad laws we've put in place or surround myself with armed individuals to protect me from harm.

On Water Rights and the Environment

Water belongs to the people as it originates from oceans and happens to land on the secured properties of the counties. The deed may have your name on it, but we can mortgage it at our leisure. The "owners" of property have the responsibility to protect water as a resource for all members of our communities.

It should be obvious to any that water needs to go where it can be of the greatest benefit. Even to the lay individual, water infrastructure needs to be created and/or maintained for the benefit of our urban centers. The needs of rural Californians can easily be satisfied by what falls out of the sky. What flows through the rivers and in the underground aquafers belong to the rest of us and the nature to which it was born.

See, man must share this precious resource with all the creatures of the earth. To artificially place man at the apex in the hierarchy of needs is short sighted and the height of hubris. It may be that man is only a waypoint in earth's history and that another creature will evolve to surpass the fleeting accomplishments we've achieved so far. Why is it we think every resource, every life is at our disposal to use as we see fit? The pure arrogance of mankind's assumption of his place in the universe is appalling. We must learn to live with all of earth's flora and fauna in an environment that is protected for the benefit of all or at least those without opposable thumbs.

Mother nature created aquafers for water storage. We have no need for dams as they impede the other creatures of the earth from returning to their birthright and creating the next generation of their species. Man should not interfere but instead learn to coexist in the environment in which he lives or move to where humans may concentrate their habitation. Nature should be left to reclaim itself without man's intervention. Let the creatures of the earth enjoy their destinies and if we are worthy we may get to share their space.

On Academics and Education

One should not be surprised when we opt to have others raise our children. Those we entrust to educate our progeny will do so in a manner and with information they chose to convey. If you're too lazy to raise the little rats, why are you shocked when they come home and tell you all about the world and what you are doing wrong and what you do not know.

You passively involve yourself with your spawn for roughly three hours each weekday evening while you turn them over to someone you don't know, hired by someone you don't know based on a set of criteria you had no input on for roughly eight hours a day. What do you think was going to return home each evening? Certainly not something that you would have intended if you'd given a damn in the first place.

We progressives welcome the opportunity to program these little biological drones into something more to our liking. 2+2 =

whatever you feel? Check. Our founding fathers a bunch of misogynists, slave owning racist pigs. Check. "Every breath you take, every move you make"[1] harms the planet and you need to pay up or be polite enough to die. Check. Gender is fluid; biology is a myth. Check and check.

Can you expect anything less than a mindless, over-opinionated creature from Stepford to invade your home at a quarter past four each evening? If this comes as a shock to you and you "long for the past", ask yourself why. You may discover that your parents gave a shit, took you to church, taught you the Pledge of Allegiance and love of country, embedded a moral code into how you were raised and generally reared a competent, functioning member of society.

Don't get me wrong, we love the fact that you just hand over those impressionable little minds to be filled with whatever dribble will meet our ends. If you ask what the hell is wrong with our kids today, just

---

[1] The Police – *"Every Breath You Take"* 1983

sit yourself in front of a mirror and let that asshole have it for willingly divesting the responsibility of raising a contributing member of the human race over to someone else. The someone else who has a long-standing agenda and knows exactly what it wants out of your kids.

What is even more mind boggling is that after grade twelve, you're willing to pay tens of thousands of dollars to even more opinionated boobs to finish them off once and for all. K-12 was just the minor leagues. Our undergrad programs in most major universities in America are littered with the finest progressive minds the real world wouldn't pay for.

As a liberal, nothing makes my heart sing more than watching a middle-class family struggle to pay those outrageous tuition fees just to have little Johnny and Janie major in English Literature. As Will Hunting from the movie "*Good Will Hunting*" stated, "you could have gotten the same education with 50 cents worth of overdue library fees." Instead of realizing they just burned $120K worth of mama and papa's money just to put on a hat with the Golden Arches emblazoned on the front and asking customers whether they wanted fries with that, they take to the streets in their hoodies and balaclavas and protest how unfair the world is and how they want their fair share.

We could not have created a more compliant set of idiots if we had bred them in a test tube. You paid us for the privilege of letting us turn your spawn into budding anarchists with little or no commercial worth in the business world.

I'm only sorry I did not invent and profit from this system. Imagine a system where you mortgage your ass to the hilt to turn your child against everything you believe, just so they can occupy your basement in perpetuity.

Please, continue to hand them over. We love it!

On Competition

Intertwined with co-opting the education system is what Sacramento radio personality Rob Williams calls "the pussification of America." This is where everyone is a winner just for participating.

Our liberal agenda has this embedded at the forefront of our indoctrination. See, it is in man's primordial nature to compete for resources, breeding partners, territory and the basic essentials to exist. By snuffing out the will to compete, society has become far more dependent on their new parent, the Government. When the will and drive to conquer has been stripped from their DNA, all that is left is a sniveling individual with their hand extended for any morsel the government is willing to provide.

How best to make society compliant? Take away the competitive spirit to create, to persevere, to challenge adversity and to build pride in one's own abilities and you'll have a dependent mass of humanity doing exactly what you tell them for the handouts to survive. For a $1.49 plastic trophy, we've created legions of pussies who truly don't know what it's like to win... or to lose.

Even to this day, I'm haunted by the times I lost the championship game and came in second place; what is commonly referred to as the first loser. It is good we spare our young from the lifelong pain and suffering that arises from coming up short. What could possibly be gleaned from that internal hell? Maybe the will and drive to perform better next time? Who really knows; they won't. 😌

On Immunizations

Yes, this is one of our more dastardly programs. Engineered to affect just a small portion of the population, immunizations can take down a few kids in each generation. In the extreme and unintended circumstance, the injections can cause death. We'd prefer a life-long impairment where the government can lend a hand or even take over for the parent in one of our fine institutions.

How else could we short circuit our way into more lives each generation? If you look at our cooption rate, we convert a fair percentage of the population to our way of government dependence using the vast array of weapons I've previously described. Shooting up kids with a random poison will accelerate those parents we normally wouldn't have touched in this generation and bring them into the folds earlier than before. Burdening independent families at random with these terrible maladies brings them closer to government. And to top it off, there is no accountability on the part of the drug manufacturer or the doctor who stored and administered the shot.

Doubling down, through legislation, we've forced parents to make a choice: immunize your children to take advantage of our eight-hour-per-day indoctrination centers (school) that you've already paid for with your taxes or lose your financial security and home school. We've forced you to play medical Russian roulette with your most precious cargo in order to let us brain wash the little cretins into something that will learn to bite back.

Take one more glance at this and absorb the true insanity of this cycle. Create and enforce a law that may be detrimental to your child, just for the privilege of coopting their education. Is this screwed up or what? Makes me proud to be part of the political structure that has the foresight to work both ends of such a twisted system.

On Invading Our Borders

Borders, we don't need no stinking borders! Seems outrageous, but why not? If mankind was meant to be together and harmonize with each other, borders directly conflict with that goal.

Regardless of whether people obey the laws, why not just turn these criminals into instant citizens once they touch foot on "American" soil? We could import the world and make citizens of each and every one. Who pays? Who cares! It's frankly the right thing to do.

America must pay for its colonial sins by opening itself to anyone and especially our neighbors to the south. If it wasn't for that crappy Mexican army that got its ass handed to it all the way back to Mexico City, Mexico would still own this land. The dream of Aztlan has never disappeared and some believe it is still within our grasp. Our progressive policies can make this dream a reality.

On the international front, we must take all displaced refugees to our bosom and let them suckle at the teat of American generosity. Disregard their abject refusal to assimilate into our society in favor of closed enclaves that reject American virtues and values that are frankly overrated.

We need not worry about a new dawn of Sharia Law on our shores. Just ask all the pink-hatted progressive women marching on DC shaking their fists at that idiot Trump demanding he let these poor and huddled 21-35 year-old battle tested males into our forgiving arms. These women obviously are more than willing to turn in their vagina hats for the comfort and style afforded by those chic burkas. One must wonder at the wisdom of our lady warriors who are so willing to flaunt the First Amendment just to get dragged all the way back into the 11th century. Now that is true progress!

There is no US without THEM

We are by far the best marketing organization on the planet. Bar none.

We've managed to align ourselves throughout American history with every evil societal scourge just to turn around and blame it on the spineless Republican Party. You name it; slavery, Jim Crow, segregation, the Ku Klux Klan; we were on the slave owning, cross burning, black man lynching side of the fence EVERY TIME but somehow managed to project our sins across the political aisle.

No big eight advertising firm could ever shed these egregious sins from our past. Not only have we purged these evils from our ledger, we've managed to reprogram America into thinking that all these things were Republican transgressions that we progressives are still battling to this day.

Multiplying miracles, we've actually got the folks we were lynching 60 years ago to vote for us on a more regular basis. If we bothered to believe in God ('cause we don't), this would truly eclipse that water to wine stunt.

On Getting Elected

With a ratio of one million to one, our so-called representative government in California is a farce, so I might as well profit from it. "Bigly."

As an incumbent, I'd be invincible. Outside of slapping the wrong ass, my sheep would blindly elect me back in perpetuity. We've seen those So Cal coastal "intellectuals" get rich, so why can't I. A job as long as I want with full pay and benefits even after I leave. The perfect con on the people of California.

And while I'm there, I can parlay my influence into tons of cash because frankly, there is never enough when it comes to money. I'll be upfront about it; I'm for sale. You want it, I'll get it done, constituents be damned. Since there are so many of them, they could never mount a challenge to me at the ballot box. But, my special interest friends will have complete access to my office, day or night as long as the price is right.

Since we all trade our souls on a daily basis, these transgressions fade with each news cycle. We will never be held accountable for our actions, indiscretions or out-right fraud and abuse of power. And if I can't collect enough coin in my name, I'll just shift it into a shell company in my wife's name. For a blueprint on how to defraud your constituents, I'll just use the Feinstein/Blumberg/High-Speed Rail model. Now that's a family who knows how to score the commas (1,000,000,000) straight out of the state treasury.

There is no US without THEM part 2

In order to win elections, we always have to be on your side.   It's just simple mathematics.

For instance, our support for women's rights gets us just over 50% of the voting population. Throw in the African Americans at 13%, Hispanics (illegal or otherwise) 24%, LGTBQ 12%, the anti-gun crowd 32%, climate change zealots 18%, and last but not least the anti-Wallstreet 99%ers.

According to our Democrat Party calculator, these effects are additive so that we have 238% of the vote in our pocket.   This guarantees our victories throughout California. If you do not believe we can garner this much of the vote, just look at the returns we received in 2016. We actually got more votes in some counties than were currently registered to vote.

The art of collecting votes by attaching ourselves to any counter cause will guarantee you'll eventually be on our side one way or another.

On Representative Government

The only way to wipe out the vote of the people is to explode the number of individuals in the Executive and Judicial branches of government. By limiting the number in the state legislature, whose primary function is to monitor the other two branches against illegal acts and bad behavior, we ensure the oppression of the People at the hands of we Oligarchs.

In our effort to ensure Native Americans and the Chinese could not vote, the Workingman's Party included inflammatory language within California's 1879 Constitution. Inserted into this hallowed document was Article XIX entitled "The Chinese". This was a set of intolerable conditions set upon the Chinese workers that basically turned those individuals into "chattel or stock" (not my words, but one of the legislators of the time.)

Not to be outdone, written into the text, only White Males and White Mexican Males (whatever the hell that looks like) 21 and older were allowed to vote.

The cherry topping on this nihilistic constitution was the cap on the membership in the Assembly and the Senate. Originally, these restrictions were placed in the constitution so that only whites would be elected to the legislature. The unintended glorious consequence of bigotry run wild was that this seeded the foundation of the Oligarchy we control and enjoy today.

Remember from before, that if we can limit the voice in the People's House, the other two branches can be coopted and grow without oversight. This is how we can create commissions and agencies that make all the rules we want to control our population (since "citizen" is such an ugly and divisive word) without the benefit of having to be voted on by the People's representatives.

Car too smoggy – fine. Live among trees – fee. Drive too much – fee. Make too much – tax. Trucks spew carbon – costly regulations. "Your" water underground – meter. Cull the population – mandatory vaccinations. Too much plastic in the landfills – fine/imprison waiters for offering a straw. Need money for our bullshit infrastructure projects – bond. Programming the youth – Common Core. Termed out legislator – create an agency to lead.

We screw up – pass.

On God

Our racist, misogynistic, slave owning founding fathers knew and stated that the Constitution would only work for a moral, God fearing, Christian society. They knew that the framework for this county would only work for a citizenry that understood their rights came from God and only a belief in Him kept these unalienable rights intact.

Cue the theme from "*Mission Impossible.*" We must wipe out God in order for your rights to come from Government. Our mission (which we've obviously chosen to accept) for the past century plus has been to belittle, berate, minimize and euthanize our belief in the Almighty.

Frankly, we've done one hell of a job! It all really starts with abortion. If we can convince a society that it is completely fine to kill children, then we can convince them of anything. Read that again. We've convinced multiple generations that it is normal to kill children. After that, any other bullshit we try to pull is purely minor league.

After killing children, everything else we trot out as normal will be normal. When the moral safeties have been removed, there is nothing that is out of bounds. Although anarchy is near to the core values we represent, someone has to be on the top. When the masses are carrying torches and pitchforks, someone has to point -> THIS WAY! In a vacuum of leadership, we will rise to rule. Sheep need to be led, but only by a select worthy few.

When God ceases to exist, Government can swoop in and provide the needed guidance, nurturing and support. Who takes care of you? Government. Who provides your meals? Government. Who provides your education? Government. Who can punish the evil rich? Government. Who can redistribute their wealth to the poor? Government. Who says who lives and who dies? Government. Where do your rights come from? Government. Who's your daddy? Government.

When the government determines who lives or dies, your Life is no longer your own. When government tells you what you can or cannot do, you no longer have your Liberty. When the government can secure its loans with your land and define what you can do with it, you have lost your Property. We have successfully removed God and your God given rights of Life, Liberty and Property. You have nothing, including your faith in the Divine.

What were the primary tenets of the Declaration of Independence? What did the Founding Fathers' put down on paper that were gifts from God? Life, Liberty and the Pursuit of Happiness (Property). All of these items are now under the exclusive purview of the Government.

Man has now substituted for God and in taking his place defines what your rights will be. Those few of us who get elected will be the overruling Oligarchy. We will determine every aspect of your miserable lives.

On Agenda 21

Let's face it; there are too many people on this planet for Mother Earth to support in perpetuity. The herd must be culled in order to let nature heal from man's infestation.

But how best remove this virus or at least lower it to a manageable level? Step one: eliminate the rural independent lifestyle and force people into large urban centers. How we do this is pure genius. Our power to tax and regulate will be the tools required to chase the vermin off "their" land.

To tax people off their property, we've developed a number of specific taxes and fees that directly impact rural residents. The fire tax (let's call it what it is, not a fee) was our direct assault on people living where we do not want. We've since traded this tax for another that will collect even more income; additional gas taxes. Based on mileage, who is impacted by fuel taxes? Those who drive great distances to perform basic tasks in their lives. How do they save money? By moving into the cities where it is not necessary to travel such long distances. See, the solutions will always be the ones we drive people towards.

If taxes are weapons in our arsenal, then the power to regulate are the nuclear options. We've given ourselves the ultimate ability to tyrannize any portion of our constituency. Let's list off some of the more onerous regulations we've put in place to drive these enemies of nature back to where we want them. 1) Water use, 2) take regulation and 3) metering. Wow, water is the basis of all life and we have total control of it!

Add on the climate change based pollution regulations, we can force these ruralites into bankruptcy. Impossible? No, highly probable. See, when the executive branch creates unelected minions that are beholden to no one, they have the ability to generate fines and fees without consequence or recourse. Paired with our police power, we can create onerous fees then arrest the owners and confiscate their property. We get to involuntarily relocate these individuals to our urban hubs which was the goal from the beginning. Oh, and by the way, the government will now own your land.

We will leave the rural population with two options: we'll make it too expensive for you to live in the wild or we'll drag you out kicking and screaming in cuffs.

Step two: now that we have everyone together, we'll just release a weaponized flu shot or some other biblical plague that will spread like wildfire with all these people stacked so tightly together. It would be a wonder if anyone actually survived.

As the corpses start stacking up, even those survivors will be hard pressed to live through the resulting disease infestation that will follow such a massive population die off.

Think I'm full of shit? Did you see the movie "*The Kingsmen*"? Was that plot so farfetched that you could not see the beauty in its design? A few that eliminate the many all to save Mother Nature. I just wish they hadn't published our playbook on film.

On Public Pensions

One sure fire way to bankrupt government is to pay its workers forever in perpetuity. (I know, "forever" and "perpetuity" mean the same thing; I did it for effect.) All on backs of the tax paying citizens (used here intentionally as "others" don't really pay taxes.)

Since our primary political backers are public employee unions, we can create a circular interdependence that puts organized crime to shame.

It works like this. The employee unions (teachers, SEIU, teamsters, UPEC, CalPERS, etc.) support our elections. We in turn boost the retirement benefits of the union members. These union members pay big bucks to their union bosses who in turn use this money to support our elections. A perfect continuous circle of ritualized fraud, waste and abuse.

But what happens when all the tax money collected goes solely to the wages and benefits of these unionized government workers? I guess we'll find out soon enough. Roads, waterways, dams (like Oroville) will all begin to crumble and fail just so these folks will get theirs. The best part of this is that the pyramid scheme is guaranteed payment by the California Constitution!

On Facts and Truth

Frankly, it doesn't matter. We decide what information is relevant or not. If our opposition comes at us with facts, we'll just shout them down. The louder we are, the more right we are.

Decades ago, we were fortunate enough to coopt the main stream media (MSM) and make it the propaganda wing of our party. With a weaponized media, we can make the irrelevant relevant and the relevant ignored. Any bullshit we manufacture can and does stay in the news cycle for as long as we deem it necessary.

"Russia! Russia! Russia!" If this is not proof positive that we can sustain an utter lie in perpetuity, I don't know what does. Compounded by the discovery that it was actually our side that was working with Russia through the deep state, we've managed to keep the 2016 election malfeasance yoked around the Republican's shoulders. Again, our sin is projected onto their ledger.

On Climate Change

This boondoggle creates the freeway to a one world order. As quickly as the seasons change, so does our rhetoric and the data that supports it. But it is important to make this a worldwide struggle so as to eliminate the recognition of borders.

How else can we discuss the important issue of our lifetime without having to deal with pesky nation states? Since air and water do not recognize borders, neither should we. It's academic that the temperature has gone up and down long before the ascension of humankind. It is only our arrogance that merits us to think we make that much of a difference.

Climate change and climate science is the silver bullet required for nation busting. If we can meet in Rio, Kyoto and Paris as ONE, we can be one People under one flag under the auspicious rulership of a select Oligarchy that wishes to enslave all seven billion on the planet. Damn, I sure as hell plan to get a seat when the music stops.

As an outgrowth of this movement, we create onerous fees, taxes and regulations. This evolution that targets a unicorn utopia (a state that can never actually come to fruition), we can move the bullseye at our leisure. If it gets warm one summer, Climate Change! If we get hit with another Nor'easter, Climate Change! If a cow farts in California's Central Valley, Climate Change! This gives us the means to create whatever domineering rules and regulations that will bend everyone to our will. Our new tools are endless, but the goals are few. World domination or bust!

On California's Constitution

Built in 1879 as the biggest racist piece of shit designed since the civil war, California's Constitution is the bedrock of what every constitution should not be. The Archivist of California, E. Dodson Wilson, stated that California's constitution was the worst in the nation.

A product of the brainchild of the Workingman's Party, this anti-Chinese, anti-Indian, anti-Mexican piece of trash is the basis of the state constitution we live under today.

We've solved some of the short comings in this document by creating and using the People's right of initiative. We've managed to change our constitution over 520 times to match the issues of today. If you've ever read this thing (I have and I'll wager you good odds most legislators haven't), you'd never be able to figure out what the hell it means. It goes back and forth, both referring to itself and to California Code which is supposed to be based on the

Constitution. Suffice it to say, it says whatever we say it does.

Speaking of initiatives, our glorious Attorney General Xavier Becerra titles these things to suit our fancy. If we don't like something and want to guarantee its failure at the ballot box, then the title will reflect a negative bent. For instance, if the People want to get rid of our new gas tax, the title of the initiative as seen on the ballot will be something like "the Transportation Destruction and Traffic Gridlock Creation Act." If we want to release tens of thousands of dangerous criminals back onto our streets, it will be titled "the Safe Neighborhoods and Schools Act." The pen, coupled with the abject ignorance of the California voter, is mightier than the sword. Words matter and if we're holding the pen, we can command your hearts and in turn your souls.

On Social Security

Social Security was the New Deal's great pyramid scheme that actually would have worked had it not been for the gross ineptitude of our federal legislators. How did we fuck this up? Let me count the ways.

1) The great borrowing extravaganza. Our wonderful legislators cannot keep their grubby little hands off pots of money that are set aside for the exclusive benefit of those who paid into the system. Instead of letting the fund grow at a modest rate of return, the feds decided to take out the cash to pay for other programs and drop IOU's in the box. This borrow and fail to repay scheme continued to shore up many progressive programs we could not normally afford.

2) Parasitic program inclusion. Tired of just borrowing from the Social Security program, the legislators began attaching non-contributing populations to syphon off the fund. Widows, orphans, handicapped

and the mentally ill; all were welcome at the trough. This got rid of the need for those pesky IOU's by taking out the money without having to pretend to pay it back at some future date.

3) Retitle the fund. This is one of my favorite shell game sleight-of-hands. Instead of recognizing that you'd paid into this supplemental retirement fund for your entire life, we now consider this an "entitlement program" and act as if you should be lucky that the government is gracious enough to give you anything at age 62 or whatever we deem the appropriate age to donate towards your standard of living in your twilight years.

4) Now we've converted this subject into a battleground issue. Remember from before, we need to have US versus THEM. Even though we've been robbing the fund blind for more than 40 years, we Dems are now committed to protecting our seniors at any cost. It is the evil Republicans who want to balance the budget on the backs of the elderly. What was it that Ebenezer Scrooge said? "Better to die and reduce

the surplus population." This also helps the health of the remainder of the fund by reducing the number of dependents the Social Security System has to carry.

Another of the cruelties we have in store is eliminating certain individuals from collecting Social Security benefits altogether. Not the illegals who are tapping into the fund without ever putting a dime into the system as that would upset our base. No, I'm referring to those greedy bastards who have been forced to put in the federal maximum into the fund for many years. It will be obvious to the average American that these people were making enough money to donate the maximum that they surely don't need or deserve to collect any at all.

Chalk up another victory for our side. We create this monster, break it six ways to Sunday then shove the entire mess down the Republican's throats and make them the bad guys when they start to reduce/eliminate benefits. This the major drawback of living in "reality-land" for Republicans; they have to figure out ways to cure our disasters. When you don't give a damn, you have the ultimate freedom to screw the pooch at will without conscience or consequence.

On the Economy

We're on cruise control now. All the battery packs are fully charged (since we don't run on carbon based cylinders anymore) and thanks to our benefactor of fiscal policy, the Big O has us running smoothly in an economic boom without end.

Thanks to his great wisdom and money management, the banks are profiting, unemployment has plummeted and wages for the first time in a long while are beginning to inch up. Never you mind that we doubled the debt to $20 trillion dollars. Realistically, we are the United States of America and will never have to pay this back. And if the notes are ever called, we'll just deed over the central part of the country which has the added benefit of getting rid of a large portion of our conservative detractors.

The not so big secret about our robust economy is that America doesn't make shit anymore. We're an almost entirely service-based economy. No tangible products, just burger flippers and sales people. Most physical products come from overseas; these same countries that are buying our debt and will be expecting payoff in the near future. I only hope they can speak Mandarin and Cantonese in Utah and Kansas.

Now that orange faced fool wants to poke the dragon and invoke tariffs that will start a trade war. By pissing off the only enemy that has huge debt markers on the US, we're going to hit the handle on the old flusher far earlier that we originally anticipated. And guess whose hand will be on the plunger? Correct again, our Republican friends will be holding the bag. It's like the Road Runner and Wile E. Coyote; in the GOP's Ignorance We Trust.

On Central Banking and the Federal Reserve

Hamilton got ripped off by being placed on only the $10 dollar bill. This founding father knew exactly how to control the nation without ever firing a shot. Too bad he got in the way of Aaron Burr's lead ball. Alexander would have ushered in monetary dominance a century earlier if he hadn't died.

His plan, which eventually took hold under Saint Woodrow Wilson, gave total control of monetary policy to an independent, for profit monopoly known as the Federal Reserve. Controlled by the Rothchilds and other banking families, this ensured that the banking system would be tightly regulated and monitored by the very people who would profit by their mischief.

The actual ability to tank the economy by raising interest rates or conversely flooding the monetary system with cash by selling bonds gives this select few the means to control every aspect of our daily lives.

Knowing when each of these handles will be pulled affords this group ultimate power. Adam Smith's market forces no longer dictate the flow of the economy, just a few mustache twisting SOBs who don't give a shit about the little people.

Too big to fail? Why yes, yes they are. When one hand is on the controls and the other on the balls of the legislature, they will never be held accountable. Who gets the short shrift? Mr. and Mrs. America always get the bill at the end of the meal. For dessert, they even give themselves multi-million-dollar bonuses for fucking everything up and all on the taxpayer's dime.

On Term Limits

I'm not sure which uneducated prick came up with idea that we could be kicked out of office based on some artificial calendar. Nice try Charly as you've now exacerbated the problem. Let me explain.

When we had our exclusive California club of 120 members and were hired for life, we all enjoyed the stability and retained the institutional knowledge of how things operated at the capitol. We even had the luxury of handing off our position to a relative or staff member who would pay us for the privilege of taking our seat. This tight little ecosystem kept the number of state funded agencies in check.

What do I mean by in check? By having been anointed with jobs for life, we did not have to create bullshit departments, agencies and regulatory bodies in which to land when we termed out. Some fool opened Pandora's Box and forced us to create a massive infrastructure of state agencies so we could continue our pursuit of perpetual public employment for life. Once on the carrousel, we never intended to get off.

If you'd just left well enough alone, your lives would not be nearly as miserable as they are today. You're all welcome to repeal this repugnant attack on your beloved servants. We promise not to hold this sleight against you. Hell, we may even get rid of some of those worthless agencies as a show of good faith as long as they're headed by Republican holdovers.

On Sanctuary State

Have you not read the 10th Amendment? It basically says that when we disagree with the federal government, we can do whatever the hell we want. Not familiar with the Constitution? I would suggest you give it a quick read so you know what you're fighting against.

California is too big to take on. With over 10% of the population, what you gonna do big man? If we've broken any laws, why are we not in cuffs? You're proving to be a toothless tiger who can't just Tweet this away. The feds will never dare to invade a state and bring it back under the boot. It's just not practicable. Go ahead, withhold federal tax money from us; we'll just stop sending it east.

Everyone knows California is a net donor state and that we'd be much better off without the rest of the country. Just for good measure, we'll take Oregon and Washington with us on the way out. We have the resources and the will to go it alone. You know we're the 7th, 8th or 9th largest economy in the world (we keep slipping for some reason) and sure as hell don't need you dragging us down.

But back to the issue at hand. Declaring our state void of following federal immigration law, we chose to protect the most vulnerable among us. Dealt an unlucky hand by being born within the wrong set of lines, we welcome these oppressed refugees into our waiting arms. We know a few of this flock are not the most upstanding of individuals, but we must understand that they are just trying to live their version of the American Dream.

By not letting our buddies from ICE know we've released a dangerous criminal back into the population, we've done our duty to mankind by helping out the downtrodden. It doesn't hurt to get another voter back on the streets. Hopefully, they can get their entire family over here as well so they can do us a solid at the ballot box.

On DACA

Come on, it's not their fault. It's their parents that dragged them here against their will. We should not take it out on them. They deserve our support, a free education, public services and any other advantage we can provide. It's their parents that are the ~~felons~~ (whoops, invading our country is only a misdemeanor) and we need to protect these angelic youth at all costs.

It is more than evident that they are truly Americans. We can see that as they exercise their freedoms under the 1st Amendment when they take to the streets and openly protest our treatment of oppressed sections of our population. We can see that when they exercise their 2nd Amendment rights when they find a handgun and it "accidentally" discharges killing an innocent woman.

We in California can prove how resilient these unwitting invaders can be. We've even appointed a young DACA illegal as head of a state agency responsible for handing out state money for college students.

These kids are American through and through, just look at all the flags they wave as they march down our streets. Red, white and blue (or is that green?) to the core.

On Welfare

This is our ultimate program to usurp control of the government. Our Founding Fathers stated that they knew the entire Republic would come crashing down if the people learned they could vote themselves money.

Well, someone has to stick up for these downtrodden masses of humanity. Our goal is to wipe out the middle class and get everyone on the public dole. Out of the sheer necessity to survive, you all have to continue to vote for us since we're the only ones compassionate enough to take care of you.

But how will we get all that money to redistribute to everyone else? Simple, we'll tax everyone into oblivion. This of course will never affect the super-rich (who are more often than not supporting these polices), but we'll tax the middle right out of existence. Romney was correct about the corner being turned, that we'd created a dependent culture of greater than 50%.

This is another of the great quandaries as to how we could have lost the 2016 election when we set everything up to run the table. California has successfully implemented this strategy as has New York. In the near future, we'll have to put Republican on the endangered species list in California. We've created a utopian mono-party where even these Republicans take loans from us just to survive. We do this so that we don't look like Russia even though we truly are.

We Democrats get elected to give more free stuff to more people. What could possibly go wrong?

On Socialism

Let's face it. Every other government that has tried Socialism has devolved into an unmitigated disaster. The problem is that the greatest minds ever assembled in one country have never given it a try. Since we are obviously the best and brightest on the planet, America and American ingenuity will get it right this time.

All other nations that have experimented with Socialism and Communism have destroyed themselves within 100 years. We are currently watching as Venezuela burns. With quintuple digit inflation, no food and no basic personal goods (it's all over when you cannot get toilet paper), Venezuela is imploding before our eyes and the world is quite content to watch but not learn.

Our Democrat prayers have been answered in the form of a young budding Socialist from New York who surprisingly destroyed an embedded swamp incumbent with the promise of free shit for all. Free college, free health care, free food, free money and no need to have a job. The perfect Utopian dream and all wrapped up in a 28-year-old idealist that has the passion to make it all happen.

Once our intellectual superiors from the Ivy League crawl out of their dank and musty halls of academia and take positions of leadership within the ruling elite, all the failures of the past will disappear like morning mist in the Sahara Desert. Since we've proven to make every impossible venture possible, America will be the one to make this work. Only idiots have attempted to reach Utopia before. With American ingenuity behind the effort, we will succeed where all others have failed.

With Americans at the helm, its people will work harder, produce more and be willing to accept an equal share of the spoils at the end of the day. In fact, the greatest mistake made by all previous attempts at nirvana was giving everyone a paycheck. This mistake we will not make. The Government will provide all food, medical care, housing (err cramped/stacked apartment ghettos), and education necessary for everyone's survival. There will be no need for money. The mistake of the past was that even the tiniest difference in pay created a jealousy between comrades that eventually brought the systems down. Without money, there will be no measuring stick for unfairness. Everyone will be equal. Everyone but we the ruling class.

By avoiding the great mistake of money, we will never run out of it or specifically other people's money. Since there will be no reason to tax as we have all the money already, our American public will kick ass and generate more food, produce more goods and live the life of communal luxury. All without the silly need for monetary exchange. As Americans, we will make this work. We never fail.

On "Insecurity"

Everything now is an "insecurity". Food insecurity, housing insecurity, health insecurity; it's all the latest buzz. And what could possibly make you feel guiltier for having a roof over your head and food on your table than us telling you about others suffering from (insert here).

Now the board is set so we can tax you for everything you've got because the less fortunate are insecure about one or more aspects of their lives. Personal choices never play a role in their current plight; the only thing that matters is that they are a "have-not" and you are a "have".

With this in mind, you'll certainly have no objections to putting out a little more so that the less fortunate can have just a taste of what you experience on a daily basis. It is the definition of "a little more" that becomes the crux of our crusade. How much is the right amount to remove all insecurities from our public at large?

Removing all insecurities would require everyone have viable housing, eliminate hunger and offer free healthcare to all. What is the price tag for this noble effort? We care not just so long as we get ours. How much should we leave you with so that you do not experience any of these situations? At the same time, we must ensure that no one, contributing to society or not, is at any time left wanting. I believe those in Eastern Europe gave this a shot in 1917.

What they found was that no matter how hard or how little they worked, they all got the basics. Competition was rendered purposeless as everyone received the same for all levels of effort. So if we take it all and return just enough for you to survive, how willing are you going to be to turn over anything in the first place? The key is to somehow find that balance between keeping you at maximum production, believing that you are getting ahead while still providing for those sitting on their asses.

Insecurity must be wiped from the planet but we must dangle enough of the carrot to keep you slogging away every day. How much will keep you a functioning member of society? 10%, 20%, 50%? That is why you hire (elect) us. We're the ones that must continually manage the mix to ensure peak output from the producers so that we may redistribute to those less likely to contribute in any meaningful way. We must go to the brink of total economic shutdown to wrangle as much out of the middle class before they become members of the lower class with their hand out trying to avoid "insecurity".

On White Privilege

Every ruling class has a rise and fall. It is past time for whitey to go down. Centuries of oppression are more than enough. It's time for the back of the bus. You're no longer welcome at the head of the table or the table at all.

All vile and evil regimes, rulers and corrupt governments share the white privilege gene. For the past two millennia, every major era came and went under the hands of white Europeans.

This continued into the 21st century but is now coming to a crashing halt. Beginning with California, we've managed to outbreed or border crash our way to the top of the census. For the first time since the Native American genocide in the 1800's, whites are now the minority in California. This trend will continue well into the future. With the numbers in our favor and white guilt on your minds, so will all the spoils follow.

We now have the ability to vote ourselves all kinds of special privileges such as free college, free food, free housing, and free medical care and finally get back at our oppressors. No longer will we be kept down. Now we will, through the laws we create, take from those who have long taken from us.

Prior to the Trump administration, the eight-year reign was the result of the great apologists who put our man in office. How better to say "I'm sorry" than to pull the lever for the non-white guy. Qualifications be damned! It was time to grovel for past sins no matter what the cost. Even if that cost was doubling our debt and shifting our country towards that of a third world shithole.

So goes California, so goes the nation. Now that California has been coopted, we'll take Oregon, Washington, New York and Massachusetts next. When Illinois and Texas fall, the reign of white terror will be over. The greatest country on the planet will no longer be run by whites. In parallel, with the middle eastern migrations into

Europe, the time of the whitewashed world will be at an end. Payback is really going to be a bitch. For a preview of what's in store, just look to South Africa as we slaughter the white farmers and steal back our land.

On Minimum Wage

Nothing levels the playing field like a mandatory minimum wage. Everyone deserves a living wage. We cannot turn our backs on the people living below the poverty line in the United States.

How is a single parent supposed to raise a family on less than $10 dollars per hour? If you use the basic formula of .50 cents per thousand, no one can live a reasonable life on $20,000 per year. If rent takes half of that, food, fuel and day care the rest, these poor and huddled masses can never break the cycle of poverty.

By increasing wages by 50%, these cornerstones of society will have the opportunity to lift themselves out of their current situation. It is the most humane policy we can institute; to help these people help themselves. But to the attentive reader, you'll realize it is not "the man" that is putting these new minimums in place. It is we who are electing those who will pander to our demands for higher wages and better living conditions.

When wages rise at such a clip, this will have an immediate effect on those recipients. If the services these folks provide (since most if not all do not produce tangible things) now cost 50% more, many will be fired and/or replaced by automatons (robots) or self-service. Remember, the big box stores have already trained us to bag our own groceries; why would they not take the next step and make us order our own food and pick it up at the counter?

The impact will be swift and unrelenting. When market forces no longer dictate the value of labor, equilibrium will again be established by reducing the workforce or replacing it with the latest technologies.

This downward cycle is not all bad as it will force these newly unemployed onto the government roles. The dependent class will ensure we get the votes to keep us in power as this will be the only way they have any chance to survive. This circular hell keeps them lined up at the ballot box to check off our names so that we give them stuff so they check off our names...

On CalExit

No state gives the middle finger to the Feds like California. Since our own constitution has been rendered irrelevant, why not the one created by those archaic founding fathers.

The plan is simple; prove the federal government is impotent when it comes to one of its own going rouge. Counter to the situation the nation found itself in the 1860's when information flowed at a much, much slower rate, we can now flip the bird at the president and see what his reaction will be. Since our Dear Leader Governor Brown is not in shackles after breaking several state and federal laws, the gloves can come off and we can swing away. The Fed's AG can sue us all he wants; but, like any spoiled child knows, if you never capitulate, you never lose control.

The 9th Circuit will protect us from any machinations the Feds can put together and hold them at bay. The nation, even though it barely tolerates our antics, will not be in any mood to have troops storm our borders and wrest control from our cabal. Riots in the streets and cities in flames just will not happen. The parallel of the North putting the South back in line cannot happen when information travels at light speed.

Gov. Brown will not retire with a whimper. With the chance at being California's president for life, he'll be willing to sacrifice all of us to attain that goal. Term limits be damned. Jerry fully intends to press his luck banking on the fact that we'll be right there to back him up.

Once we call their bluff, we'll pass legislation based on the 9th and 10th Amendments and remove ourselves from this tainted union and go our separate way. As the (let's say) 8th most powerful economy in the world, we'll have the actual authority to make treaties and deals with foreign powers, champion climate change, green energy and join the one world order, I mean United Nations. As a sovereign nation, we'll even be able to build a wall to keep out those from the east as we welcome our brothers and sisters from the south.

The CalExit initiative will provide just another javelin to try and spear the eagle. If this idea passes, then it proves that we no longer want to be part of this archaic institution and that we'd be better off going it alone.

There is one tiny little problem with our formula. There are pockets of resistance to our way of life (basically 80-90% of California's land mass) that hate our guts and would prefer staying with the nation. The most formidable group out there is the State of Jefferson folks which we've successfully ignored and kept out of our press. These Jeffersonians have been at it for over five years and just won't go away. There is a high likelihood that when we break away they won't go easy. That's why it is imperative that we strip them of their assault weapons, pistols, shotguns, knives and sling shots long before the secession from the union takes place.

On Victimhood

How can we ride in as knights to save the day without having our proverbial damsel in distress? We must charge in to save somebody, but who? This is where victimhood comes in.

Democrats are experts in battling for the little guy, the underdog, the downtrodden. So why not battle for everyone! Just name it and I'll throw a label on it, define the prescribed offense and who perpetrated this evil deed. Let's give this a try.

Blacks – putting our people in bondage for profit - white slave owners. Homelessness – unequitable distribution of resources – the rich one-percenters. LGTBQ – scorned alternative lifestyles – arrogant bible thumping Christians. Women – 50.2% of the world's population – toxic masculinity and men in general. Illegal aliens – border jumping, Rio Grande swimming felons – privileged citizens trying to protect what's theirs. Climate Change – Mother Earth suffers under the effects of industrialization

– climate deniers, reputable scientists and reasonable people. Murdered high school students – innocent bystanders that were slaughtered – the NRA, gun culture, and 2nd Amendment misinterpreters.

The list is endless and the marches can proceed nonstop. It is our duty to protect and promote the causes of each of these special classes of individuals who have one thing in common. Oppression. What do we gain? Us versus Them. And as you know, we're always on YOUR side.

On Sue and Settle

How the hell are we going to pay for all this ruckus we cause? That's easy, we'll make the same folks we're going after pay the bill. Impossible? No. We actually do this on a daily basis.

Class is now in session.

Let's use our friends at the Environmental Protection Agency as our patsy. The EPA is comprised mostly of our supporters who are out hunting down companies that they believe are adversely affecting the planet. Now when they do not act or react fast enough for our liking, one of our many green warrior groups will gin up a federal law suit against the EPA. Of course, the EPA agrees with the suing party so they capitulate and proclaim their guilt. Now the courts (who are also in our pocket) join the dance and level a hefty fine against the EPA or the EPA just "settles" the case as well as paying for the outrageous fees of our winning litigating team.

So let's recap. One group sues their friends who admit guilt and pays their friends with YOUR money. Oh, I didn't mention that? Yes, this perpetually fraudulent circle is all financed with YOUR tax dollars. The EPA should retitle itself so as to have the letters ATM because that is what we use this system for.

What do we do with all that cash we just rung out of John Q. Public? We hire more lawyers to create new cases in which to sue our friends in the federal government. Our morals may be bankrupt but our funding schemes are endless.

On Antifa

Every army has to have soldiers and what better way to engage our unemployed/ underemployed youth. We've managed to coopt an entire restless generation by pointing to "the man" and pinning a label on him.

If you do not agree with us you're a Fascist. Pure and simple, no arguments to be had. Believe that a 35-year-old man cannot put on a dress and walk into the little girl's restroom – Fascist. Expressing your 1st Amendment rights that are not in line with our thinking – Fascist. Conservative outspoken homosexual – Fascist. 2nd Amendment advocate – Fascist. Police – Fascist.

What's a Fascist? According to the American Heritage Dictionary, 4th Addition:

"fascism (făsh'ĭz̧əm) n. A system of government marked by centralization of authority under a dictator, stringent socioeconomic controls, suppression of the opposition through terror and censorship, and typically a policy of belligerent nationalism and racism."

Ok, now that we have a base on which to pivot, let's proceed. Begin with dressing like the North Vietcong, our soldiers wear all black and hide their faces behind Balaclavas threatening to burn whatever city they happen to be invading at the time. We make these threats to ensure you cannot speak your mind on the pain of bodily harm or death. *Suppression of the opposition through terror and censorship*, check.

Now we align ourselves with Black Lives Matter which gives us carte blanche to do whatever to whoever we want. If you disagree, you're a racist. But using race as a weapon can go both ways. *Typically a policy of belligerent racism*, check.

Who are our soldiers? The unemployed/underemployed youth of our nation. What do they want? What you've got. How do they get that? By creating an environment where they can redistribute what you have amongst themselves. *Stringent socioeconomic controls*, check.

Who is financing all this discord? Basically, it's George through many different tax-exempt entities. They all have one thing in common, to get to a one world order where they become the few oligarchs running the show. *Centralization of authority under a dictator*, check.

The circle is now complete. As stated before, we project every evil upon our enemies with the label we have earned and deserve. We are the Fascists!

On Merit Based Immigration

Every living human being on the planet qualifies to be in America. That is all the merit that is required.

In earlier times of America's history, we used to have to bring "something" to the table before we were allowed to gorge upon its bounty. A skill, a trade, an ability that would be valuable to the melting pot is all that was required to be welcomed as one of the tired, poor and huddled masses.

Clearly, that type of system cheated America of the additional resources that today we call votes. If you were industrious, willing to work hard and had a marketable skill, the gray lady welcomed you to our shores. And once you achieved the American dream, who were you going to vote for? A schmuck like me who wants to take it all away and give it to someone else so I can buy their vote?

Without any redeeming qualities, we politely passed. But no more! Everyone is welcome. We'll provide food, medical, housing and an education, all for free! All we require is that you continue to vote for those who provide you with the aforementioned trinkets of our appreciation. You don't have to like us, respect us or frankly, know what the hell we are doing as long as you keep us in power.

On USA – World Police

This is one of our shining achievements throughout history. We big, we bad, and no other wannabe tinpot dictator wants to mess with the USA. Who better to be the world's nanny but for the group that was founded on Judeo-Christian values?

Look at the world today. Who else should be correcting the morals of the rest of the planet? Who else can you trust with that awesome responsibility? Who's stupid enough to drain their treasury and destabilize their own economy just to keep two warring factions apart in a war that spans millennia? You guessed it. Murica.

We are number one in the world for many reasons, especially our omnipotent presence around the globe. We've managed to piss everyone off so many times it is hard to count. The one thing that does not jive with our tainted reputation is why we continue to be the number one destination for every fleeing reprobate around the planet. All dreamers desire our shores even though we've probably kicked the crap out their prior country or at least destabilized it enough to warrant their coming to America.

After all we've done to "support" the world, people still make this their primary refuge, invited or not.

On The United Nations

Our grand excuse to butt-in everywhere we're not wanted. But since we pay the tab, why the hell not. Dressed in powdered blue, just for you, we circle the globe on various peacekeeping missions to save the world from itself.

The end game of it all is to have only one viable peacekeeping force, paid for by "We the People", but run by the globalist oligarchs. We will cull the herd down to the appropriate half billion progressives worthy of calling mother earth home. The rest of y'all will go the way of the dodo bird. It will take decades to pull this off, but we've proven to be a very patient bunch. We're only into this thing for about 135 years so we have plenty of stamina. It will take probably twice that to get to the end game. A one-world order for only the most worthy. I'll send you a postcard when I arrive.

On The Uranium One Deal

Of all the mischief our leadership pulled off, this is likely the most heinous. Our buddies at the Arkansas C Corp (aka the Clinton Clan) while SecState, managed to sell off one quarter of our uranium reserves to our cold war adversary.

How we managed to tag team this one is anyone's guess but the effects and ramifications haven't even begun to be felt. This is equivalent to one of the Hatfields selling their powder and shot to the McCoys. You just don't do it.

You'll never be able to say we Democrats aren't a greedy bunch. Like our votes in the legislature, we're always for sale. This time, we really stretched our morality and sold our souls to the devil himself. Crazy thing, as always, we do this in the daylight and don't give a shit what anyone thinks. If there is money to be made, country be damned.

Now, I'm sure you figured out by now that C Corp wasn't the only one scraping cash out of this deal. But since we own the DoJ, you'll never really know whose pockets got lined in the deal. (Hint: probably a guy born in Kenya)

On Three Californias

Brilliant! That Silicon Valley tool has managed to come up with a plan to magnify our mischief. Instead of trying to secede from the union, why not just take over the federal government through mitosis. (For those who were not paying attention in biology and were concentrating on raging hormones, mitosis is the creation of identical cells through division.)

In this way, we can create three progressive states from one. Once those stabilize, we can do it again and again. Since we'll dominate the Senate, other blue states can reproduce this model and create two Illinois', two New Yorks, two New Jerseys, two Connecticuts and so on. When we take back both houses (and we always do), we'll be able to dominate the political landscape forever. Gerrymandering will be child's play compared to this little gem. After the dust settles, we'll never lose another election. Just like the feckless Republicans in the California statehouse, so will the federal congress become.

And just for good measure, we'll be able to welcome Puerto Rico into our bosom and get another bushel of progressives hungry to feed at the trough of American generosity. To show our gratitude for all those votes, we'll even pay off their debt so they can have a fresh start in their first year of statehood.

On Water Storage

Water is the key element of life and as such we must control every drop of it. Meter it, tax it, waste it; it matters not what we do with it as long as we maintain control.

During our recent five-year "drought", we managed to flush so much fresh water out to sea in the guise of saving the now extinct Delta Smelt that we successfully created an artificial water shortage. The kabuki dance of bullshit conservation measures immediately ensued. Every other day watering depending on the last digit of your home address, draconian fines for watering the sidewalk, convincing the sheeple that it is not necessary to flush all the time. We were literally turning Northern California into a cesspool. Yes, you read that correctly. The ones who actually had the water were forced to save like never before just so those in Southern California could continue to water their lawns without prejudice.

Those in Northern California became so adept at conserving water that the water companies were starting to go broke. To prevent that tragedy, the CPUC allowed the water companies to raise their rates to recover the lost revenue. I know what you're thinking and you're correct; the folks are now paying the same amount of money for up to 30% less water.

Meanwhile, out at the ballot box, Guv Brown convinced the masses that the only way to prevent California from turning into the vast wasteland it normally is without piping water all over the place was to put up for vote a seven-billion-dollar water bond. As usual, the uninformed masses (my kinda people), bit on the line of BS and passed the bond measure. Most of that money was channeled into the general fund but the unused portion remains idle. Not one additional drop of water was saved even though we managed to pile more debt onto our grandchildren.

The Sites Reservoir has been waiting for generations for construction to begin. Now that Edmund is ready to jump into forced retirement, guess where his family's 2,700 acres is? Right again, in Colusa County where the Sites Reservoir will be built. Anyone willing to take odds on who will become the state's largest pot farmer? Me neither.

There is one more solution that Moonbeam is attempting to pull off to fulfill daddy's dream of providing all the water Southern California needs at the expense of the north. This scheme is called the Delta Tunnels. We spin this project by saying we're saving the environment by controlling the salinity of the delta when we actually plan to drain that sucker dry. Putting two massive concrete straws in one end of the state to feed the other would never have a negative effect, would it? If you wonder who holds the strings on this puppet, it is our brethren in LA.

If you've ever wondered what political power looks like, just refer to the county that would have the 10th largest population in the US if it were a state. With 15 of 40 of the state's senators and 24 of the 80 in the assembly, they rule with an iron fist.

Nothing is beyond their reach and their reach is all the way up into the reservoirs of Northern California.

On Blue Lives Matter

No, they don't. We need something to rail against and the primary focus of our angst is the uniformed people's army. An unwieldy group of out-of-control lawmen who exist only to torture, maim and kill minorities.

Nothing gets the folks into the streets like a thug taking two in the back fleeing from the scene of some crime. It is amazing how angelic these poor gentlemen of color become once the news of their "untimely" demise hits the press. One must wonder at life's daily pressures that made them wander into their first foray of crime while being unlucky enough to fall at the hands of the bloodthirsty men in blue.

It matters not that one could wallpaper a house with their rap sheets; the shooting was unjustified and we need a reason to burn the city to the ground. Get on the balaclavas, paint up your signs and respond to Soros' Craigslist ads for rent-an-anarchist because it's time to march and bring "the Man" down.

This is what we're best at. Create a controversy, gin up the violence and then act as the peacemaker, all the while dividing the people and generating as much strife as possible. No one fuels the flames of anarchy like we progressives do. How else can we manage chaos if we don't stir it up in the first place? Never one to let a crisis go to waste, we'll be there to shut down the greater metropolitan area until you meet our demands. They vary from situation to situation but always end in us being in control. If we can call off the dogs and are holding all the dog whistles, you will remain terrified putty in our hands.

Cops become an unwitting pawn in a grander game of power and control. Unfortunately, this includes collateral damage, especially when some of our more zealot members cowardly sneak up on a squad car and snuff out the occupants. Our only blue line between the rule of law and the apocalyptic version of Mad Max is marginalized to the point of become the public's enemy. Of course, that is, until someone is breaking into *your* crib.

On The Electoral College

How can the people ever govern the way the masses desire unless we get rid of that archaic method of electing our highest leaders? What possibly could our founding fathers been thinking when they created such a system that would thwart the will of the people?

Surely this anachronism must be abolished to make way for the people's wishes to be heard. Why did they put this system in place? Is it not better to collect the focused will of the ten largest metropolitan areas and let them determine how the entire country should be governed? Why shouldn't 317 square miles laud over the 3.8 million square miles of these United States? It would seem only reasonable that those who have learned to live in close concentrated quarters would best be in a position to judge how others should thrive. If we can harmoniously pack thousands of people into one square block, it is natural to assume these people are of superior intellect and would inherently select the most worthy among us to lead the nation.

We lost the 2016 election because of this prisoner to time. By over 1.5 million votes, we would have kept the party rolling for another four years. Come to think about it, the party never would have stopped as we would never have lost another election. The only thing keeping us from our rightful place on the throne is those pesky fly-over states that have more guns than brains. Just give us both houses of Congress one more time and we'll fix this system once and forever.

On Water Meters

This is our weak attempt to raise taxes on rural residents. Our real play is to institutionalize the fact that you do not own your land. By placing meters on something that you own and charge you for something that belongs to you, we are cementing the fact that you are our bitch.

Sure, we'll tell you that we are trying to save the environment by ensuring that you do not take more than your fair share, but our ultimate goal is to make it so expensive, so onerous that we force you off your property. As a side benefit, we'll be able to come on to your property anytime we wish in the guise of enforcing compliance. Fourth Amendment be damned! We'll come check out what you're doing just because we feel like it. And if by chance we find out you're doing anything else we do not approve, we'll call in our buddies to raid your place and shut you down.

Want your property back? We'll claim that you're illegally storing some nebulous item and confiscate your property and sell it based on the assumption that you benefitted from the illegal storage. You may not even be charged with a crime, but we'll take it anyway. Think we can't do this? Just ask your local drug kingpin and see how it worked out for him.

With all this hassle, would it not just be easier to move into one of our lovely stack and pack houses in one of our overcrowded cities? The water flows freely from the tap and you need not worry about the alphabet soup agencies pounding on your door making sure you're complying with our myriad of rules and regulations.

On The FBI and Department of Justice

How to begin? This situation rewrites itself daily. The big takeaway here is that we are completely out of control. We've weaponized our most trusted departments of government (the G-Men and the Department of Justice) for personal embellishment. Since we were a shoe-in to win the 2016 election, none would have been the wiser and this never would have seen the light of day.

Oops! Guess we did not figure on the one guy impervious to outside influence and control would actually beat our heir apparent. Not only did he call his shots during his campaign, he's continued to look like the Oracle at Delphi with his continuous correct predictions on our malfeasance. Russia be damned; it was we who were playing fast and loose with foreign governments. When all the cards are shown on the table, the involvement at all levels of government will be so broad, so wide that the shock will deliver the public impotent.

Americans are not willing to believe what is truly in front of their eyes. To admit that the corruption was so complete and widespread, "We the People" would have to accept the realization that we put these assholes in power. They kept these assholes in power and now we have to forgive these same assholes so as not to accept blame for our original sin: putting these assholes in office. The mind is a tricky thing; it can be convinced of anything as long as it will not bring damage to its host. Letting these assholes walk will be the only "rational" course of action. To think or believe otherwise would mean that the entire fabric of our Republic is a lie, our government is a sham and something would have to be done.

With the aid of our diligent programming, America is complacent and willing to accept all the evils hoisted upon her. To reject these fools would require a considerable amount of action and that is something she is not prepared to do. The 2nd Amendment was placed inside our Constitution for this very moment, but we are not up to the challenge. We are weak; we just want our participation trophy and to go to the pizza parlor for a couple of hours pretending everything is ok, which it clearly is not.

America is a banana republic 135 years in the making. We just do not have the intestinal fortitude to look in the mirror and call ourselves out. Any imaginary literary work at this point would have DC in flames along with the routes to those 10 square miles lined with the guilty impaled upon pikes. Instead, we'll just watch the insanity for a couple of minutes, wag our fingers or tongues stating "someone" should do something about all this corruption before turning the channel to the game.

You'll never be that "someone", and that is something on which we politicians rely. The impotent complacency of the American public is a guarantee we bank on when we try to (and mostly succeed in) pulling this shit. Even when uncovered, most just choose to believe there is nothing to see here and close their eyes to the collapse of their own nation.

To believe otherwise would require one to take action, to rise as the founding fathers had, to take up arms and correct all that stands before them. Hell, the founding fathers even legalized it, codifying it in the 2nd Amendment. We've been given the right to abolish the government if it does not suit our needs. We're counting on the fact that you won't. We always have. Why not just go back to the fridge and grab another beer? The second half kickoff is about to begin.

On Security versus Privacy

Go ahead, guess where I stand on this one. Ah, you got it, security reigns supreme. Security gives us the right to blow through as much of the Bill of Rights as we wish, all in the guise of making everyone safe.

I once read that Privacy was not in the Constitution, the author even asking his readers the question if it should be included and what would such an amendment say. That idiot was dead wrong. It falls under Property Rights and the right to property enjoyment is in the Constitution. So now we have the competing goals of Property versus Security.

Since one of our goals is to make property rights minimal if not altogether eliminated, one of our best devices would be to ensure that everyone is safe. Safety and security will require cameras on every street corner, in every business establishment, in every school and certainly in every government venue. Now the tough part. How to get people to voluntarily wear cameras and listening devices on themselves where ever they go? Just to hide the subterfuge, we should also figure out a way to make them pay for the privilege.

On top of fooling the public into traipsing around in wearable tech, we must also convince the sheeple that they need digital assistants at home to handle their every command. Turn on the lights, shut off the fan, play music; these devices do it all for you. The only caveat is that they are listening to you 100% of the time in order to respond at a moment's notice. All speech is translated, stored, interpreted and then analyzed to see if they have a need to respond. All this is traversing the Internet. And big brother is listening. Alexa, can you help shatter my illusion of privacy?

For our final feat of privacy elimination, we'll stop teaching cursive writing in school so that all correspondence will go through that new-fangled Internet thing. This way we can review ALL communications to determine if they are detrimental in any way to the American Public. We'll shroud them in something really cool sounding like the Patriot Act (for who isn't a patriot) and spy on Americans all the time. Artificial Intelligence is far enough along to process all communications at light speed and alert our most trusted government servants if anything is amiss in the electronic ether.

Ben Franklin (yes, that old womanizer) once stated that, "those who would give up essential Liberty, to purchase a little temporary Safety, deserve neither Liberty nor Safety." Well Ben, betcha didn't think we'd ever progress to this point of the brink. We've allowed our government to surveille us 24/7/365 and we've even introduced gadgets into our own homes to complete the process. For the "good" of the nation, we'll be installing some audio/visual devices to keep you safe, just like we did when we required everyone building a new home to install sprinkler systems. And lest we forget, you'll be paying for these devices so we can spy on you, you kinky bastard. Now if we could only jack into your dreams…

On Transportation

How many times have you allowed us to tax you for the same thing and not produce any results? Triggers have been embedded into the California Constitution that require the legislature to provide certain monies for road and infrastructure projects. The legislature ignores the California Constitution as easily as they ignore federal supremacy over immigration.

Let's be frank. We want you out of your fucking cars. We want you living within a five-block area riding to work, school or the store on your little mono-speed bike. If we're to get you to save this planet, we have to make the roads impassable.

Now, the only way to get you on your bike and out of those carbon fouling machines, is to let the roads crumble into disrepair. You should not have any real need to travel beyond your little hovel.

And we promote this through regionalism. That's what a COG is; a Council of Governments. These were developed to snarl traffic and cripple the people's ability to traverse from one place to another all in the name of beautification and urban renewal. If you cannot get from point A to point B, why not just park it and walk or ride your bike. We've designed and created these perfect living spaces that foment your trapped, immobile lifestyle created just for you and yours. Go to the next COG meeting in your local region and see what we've planned for your community. We consider you part of our ant farm; act accordingly.

On Environmental Justice

Protecting the environment is our number one priority on the planet. It even supersedes the needs of the humans infesting this globe. Regardless of impact or cost, environmental protection is the only valid reason to run for office.

If we make the planet unlivable, then we doom ourselves to a preventable destruction. We have the power to change the way we live, work and recreate. In all of these endeavors, we must put the planet first. This will require many sacrifices which we should all be willing to pay. And pay dearly you will. (Bwahahahaha....)

The past few decades have shown that humans left to their own devices cannot be trusted to take on this awesome responsibility. Therefore, we must step in and guide you through this great endeavor. We will help you achieve this lofty but necessary goal of saving the planet for future generations.

We have myriad ways to help heal Mother Earth. The first arrow in our quiver relates to rules and regulations. We will fine, fee and tax your ass into submission. We will create such onerous regulations that the only way to capitulate to our demands is by paying up. Carbon credits anyone?

The second method is to enrage indigenous peoples into crushing any usable infrastructure into dust. Can you say Klamath Dams? Yes, four perfectly good, clean energy hydroelectric dams will be destroyed so the local tribe can once again fish for salmon. Never mind that the salmon have never travelled that far upriver or that the tons of sediment at the base of those dams will poison the waters for decades; we're trying to save the planet here.

I love the third plank in our platform. Use the children! How could anyone look at a tender five-year-old (and I'm not talking to you Podesta) and not want to wipe away their tears for fear that their planet will be uninhabitable by the time they reach adulthood. What type of an uncaring, selfish SOB would you have to be not to be out there shielding these children from the awful fate of an unlivable planet?

Our fourth technique is good, old-fashioned guilt. Come on, you had that mother too. If you have even one shred of goodness in you, this method will devastate you. Do you remember that old commercial of the Native American looking at all that garbage with the tear in his eye? Talk about linking up methods two and four into a powerful message. I even felt guilty and I've never thrown shit out the window of a moving vehicle in my life. That there are so many people like me is the reason this method works so well. Even at my minimalist attempt to be environmentally savvy, I'm still an ardent recycler. That is why guilt is so powerful; unless you're a sociopath, it works!

One of our last schemes is to employ college radicals. No one could ever defend destroying the planet. Giving these kids a softball to hit out of the park will embolden them to pick up more dicey causes in the future.

On Protecting Endangered Species

The spotted flying bucked-tooth squirrel is a regal beast worth saving. Never heard of this champion of the forest? Does it even matter to us if you've never heard of it? This majestic squirrel exists because we say it does. And since it is so rare that even the imagination cannot conjure an image of what it looks like, it obviously requires our protection.

We will protect this beast at all costs. First by determining its natural habitat and then by declaring all the lands within a thousand miles a protective sanctuary. Even if this new footprint includes your property. You are now infringing upon one of nature's little creatures therefore your land is forfeit. Because you invaded this poor animal's home, we will not give you a dime for what was "your" property. In fact, we're more likely to arrest you for all the harm you've done while in adverse possession of this creature's domain.

Sound crazy? Just ask the ranchers of Northern California about the Canadian Grey Wolf. A wolf who's never even been to California was given free range of the wilds in an area it has never roamed. Seven of these beasties were outfitted with electronic collars so that California Fish and Game (yes, that is their name in the California Constitution, no matter what they retitle themselves) so that they can be tracked to ensure that humans do no harm to them. If they stop moving, some son of a bitch is going to pay. Regardless of the number of livestock they slaughter, these killing machines have total control wherever they choose to roam. Bizarre behavior like wholesale slaughter of an entire heard cannot bring a stop to this madness. Touch one of these wolves and life as you knew it is at an end. These ranchers are now left defenseless. Best that they keep to our script, sell off what's left of their herd and property and head to the comfort of the city. Here they just don't have to deal with issues like these. Isn't that the plan all along? ;)

On Protecting our Forests

One could not protect the fauna without protecting the flora or in this case the forests of California. We've instituted such strict policies that no one is allowed to manage the forests any longer. This has multiple benefits as I will now explain.

Begin by remembering that job one is getting people out of the forests and into the cities. By restricting logging to near zero, we will eliminate the jobs related to the logging industry. All these folks have abandoned their roughneck lifestyles for jobs in the cities. All the mills are idle, trucks are rusting and timber is now imported from Canada. A renewable resource is actually brought in from a foreign country.

If that did not chase them off then this surely will. By ensuring that no one can touch the forests, we'll guarantee that they become overgrown, while the forest floor is littered with combustible material. When the lightening strikes or the winds smash the power lines together, fires will ignite, then burn baby burn. It's tough to live in an area that has been burned to the ground for miles in every direction. Best get that one car load of memorabilia out before it all gets erased from the face of the earth. I'm guessing that you lived in such a remote area that your house became uninsurable in the past few years. Now you've lost everything without the ability to rebuild. Again, best to run off to the safety of the cities where shit like this never happens.

Funny thing about letting all this timber go up in smoke. One acre of burned forest puts as much carbon into the atmosphere as 770 cars running 24 hours a day for a year. Chasing these rural residents off their land sure comes at a steep environmental cost, but hell, it's worth it.

Author's note: I wrote this months before the Camp Fire tore through the Paradise community just I was going to press. I did not alter the text as callous as it may seem. Being right does not make this any easier. May they rest in peace.

On Enhancing Sustainability

No one really knows the awesome power in the word Sustainability. It is a word that goes unquestioned as it represents the highest ideals of humankind. So naturally, we've co-opted it as our own.

Everything now revolves around sustainability. You cannot do anything without it having some sustainable aspect to it. Or in the extreme, if you want to do something that is not sustainable, you'll have to pay an environmental "sin" tax in order to do it. Want to build a new runway for your airport? Then buy ten times the required acreage of swampland/desert/ lunar landscape somewhere close by and turn it into "habitat." You'll pay dearly for this into eternity. And you'll be paying dearly to one of us for the privilege to grow your economy. Because without paying the ferryman, no one is getting to heaven.

We've now created myriad commissions and agencies to set up rules and regulations, fines and fees and for the truly lucky ones, jail time. All available to those trying to successfully dance to our tune of saving the planet. Light bulbs, plastic bags, solar panels and electric cars; the list is endless and therefore so is our reach into your lives.

But hey, we all want to be good stewards of the environment. Sustainability is such an overused word although it is much better than "bend over and get ready to take it up the ass because here is our new set of regulations." It has fewer letters too!

On Alternative Energy

This is one of my favorites. The myth of green energy. Outside of hydroelectric power which is clean and efficient, but we're out to destroy that one. Every other source of green power has a major gotcha attached to it.

Wind power: ever heard of a frog in a blender? Well, this is the avian version of the same concept. Birds managed to get whacked by the blades of these bad boys on a much too frequent basis.

Solar power: those large black panels remain hugely inefficient as energy collectors. They come with a really cool catch-22. If you live in an area with a lot of sun, you probably have little rain so the panels are constantly getting covered with dirt and grime which limits the efficiency of collecting the sun's rays. If you live in an area with enough rain to keep your panels clean, the clouds block the sun's rays and lower the power output. It's also worth mentioning that it takes 25% of the energy created over the panel's lifetime to produce it in the first place.

Electric cars: whoa! Those are some really big batteries you have Elon! All the better to pollute the environment my dear! Remember how you've been Pavlovian trained to never throw away a battery in the garbage? Well, what the hell are you going to with that 500-pound Enercell in your front yard? Better still, it costs more to hook up your little Prius in time and electric consumption than it does for good old carbon-based transportation. Which leads me to my next epiphany; most of the electricity generated today is carbon-based as well. So we sacrifice precious time and money to serve our planet by buying into more carbon spewing electrical plants all to warm ourselves in our own smug cloud. (You need to get out more: South Park, Season 10, Episode 2)

On Unemployment Benefits

The key to retaining votes has always been the circular relationship between a Democrat incumbent and a person's next meal. If you prefer to sit on your ass and collect a check, all we require of you is to check off the box next to the guy with a "D" by his name. You get free stuff and so do we.

Nothing brands a Republican as a harsh son of a bitch like the promise of cutting unemployment benefits for the poor. The only time you can get away with this tactic is if your district is so affluent your only true electoral challenge is in your party's primary. Otherwise, you might as well drag a knife across your throat. Being that heartless guarantees your personal destruction at the ballot box. The best a Republican can do in a contested district is to say nothing at all.

Of course, that leaves the entire conversation on our side of the house. We can promise the moon (delivering is another thing) and it makes for good sound bites. Yes! We will increase your weekly benefits! Yes! We will extend your time on the dole. Yes! We'll pretend you're looking for work! Yes! You can continue to breed and receive even more!

There is never an ending point when spending other people's money. We take it from you and give it to them so they can put us back in office to repeat the cycle again. Benjamin Franklin said, "When the people find that they can vote themselves money that will herald the end of the republic." The doomsday clock is ticking...

On The Destruction of Prop 13

Unwinding this little gem is going to take some time. In a rare instance of public revolt, the people of California in 1978 managed to cap their property taxes at 1% of transacted/assessed value at time of sale with a 2% per annum escalator. A bold move for a relatively feckless population.

The only way to take down this cash starving blight on our Constitution is to chip away at it. We've already instituted bogus "fees" on certain properties such as the "Fire Fee." This had limited success as a test balloon but we had to try for something on a grander scale.

In order to do this, we had to pull the same old rabbit out of the hat: frame the issue as rich versus poor. I know, trite, but it always works. We've conjured up the illusion that "rich" companies are not paying their fair share of property taxes. So, anyone filing as a corporation (any type) will be split out of the Prop 13 protections and be reassessed at market rates. No more frozen valuations. As the economy heats up, so will the tax revenue.

Once everyone is used to a "split role" Prop 13 application, we'll reassess when a family member dies and leaves property behind. And then expand to any family event be it death, marriage, divorce, new phone number, etc. We'll get the party going all over again. Somehow, we'll have to convince everyone that this was the evil Republican's doing; we always project our sins across the aisle.

On The Financial Burden of Higher Education

For those who can't afford it, we'll give it away for free especially if you came to this country illegally. For everyone else, we'll hoist upon our youth the yoke of perpetual poverty in the form of student loans. Who owns the student loans? That's right, your Daddy, the government.

Every attempt to escape our grasp will come to naught. You'll eventually be beholden to Uncle Sam one way or another. It's to our advantage that we rope you in young and keep you under the boot for as long as possible. Your only hope of escape will come in the form of some sort of amnesty so that we can legislate your debt away. Of course, there'll be some conditions on your release such as working for government for a certain amount of years or becoming a teacher. Because the more teachers we have, the lower wages will be which will make them more dependent on other government services.

The goal is to always come back to your Daddy in one form or another. As long as you're a dependent of government, you'll have to vote for those who are willing to give it all away to you.

The crazy thing about student debt is the reason to chase the sheepskin in the first place. We've flooded the airways with all the poverty and homelessness we could possibly gin up. The remedy to those young, impressionable minds was to get a good education to keep from being on the streets.

No one has $120,000 dollars just lying around so we create the myth of help through FAFSA and other bullshit screening programs that will let you know how much help we can give. Poor as dirt, welcome to your free ride. Member of the middle class, you won't get a dime unless you're willing to pay it back at some future date. Way back when, we called that indentured servitude. Today, we call it Democrat Party building. As the ones who trapped you in this menagerie, we're the only ones who can release you from this bondage.

And why is the debt so high? Because someone has to pay for all that brilliance that the real world would not. Professor and administrators (some of our most ardent supporters) need a different type of government welfare. And they do fair well. Their salaries are outrageous. Without the student loan programs, the entire collegiate scam would collapse since a free market would not pump this type of money into the system. It has to be subsidized or it simply would not exist.

On My Mentor – Barry O

Who was the one political figure that had the greatest impact on me? It was none other than number 44, the man, the legend in his own mind, the dude way too smart for the rest of us. Barry Soetoro.

The culmination of all the white guilt in the northwestern hemisphere resulted in hiring a socialist community organizer as our first black president. We felt so guilty that we actually did it twice just to prove there was not a shred of prejudice left in this nation.

My mentor was hired with no particular skill set accept a mild gift of gab and the unwavering ability to appear to be your intellectual superior. Just ask him, he'd tell you so. A condescending prick with a huge agenda of not so much hope but plenty of radical change. HE was the one, our Neo, our messiah. A man lacking any marketable skills but blessed with enough melatonin that he could get away with literally anything. Congress, who needs them. He had a pen and a phone and lacked the knowledge or decency to obey the Constitution.

How could such an individual not be my hero, my Zen Master, my Yoda. To take all the advantages of race and parlay it into a career that fostered racial hatred and divide was truly inspiring. He proved that anything was truly possible in America including the ability to tear it apart from the inside out. Abraham Lincoln said, "America will never be destroyed from the outside. If we falter and lose our freedoms, it will be because we destroyed ourselves." Amazing how much of a crystal ball many of our former presidents had.

The "Great Divider" proved that anyone could become president and that should inspire us all. He single-handedly brought identity politics to the next level.

On The Media

The Fourth Estate was once the conscience of the American experience. Luckily for us, we bought most of it. Now it serves our Democrat Party as our propaganda wing. We really have no need for campaign advertising any longer. All that is required is a clandestine meeting and the "truth" is ushered forth on page one for as long as we wish.

Russia, Stormy, and children ripped from their parents and sent to detention centers. The headlines vary, but it always remains bad news for the Republicans. There is no objectivity from our mainstream media anymore. An early example of bad behavior was the yellow journalism of Hearst around the turn of the 20th century. Hearst was able to gin up a war via his reporting. From there we've progressed to the point where news does not exist, opinion is stated as fact and inciting riots and mayhem is all in a day's work.

Although Antifa is the armed insurgency of our party, the great mind fuck comes from our friends at CNN, MSNBC, ABC, CBS, NYTimes, WaPo and the like. Where once Walter Cronkite delivered our daily dose of dealings around the world, his protégé Dan Rather tried to crush a president with falsified information. Although castigated for his role in attacking Bush, Danny opened the door to weaponizing the media for future generations.

Nothing we see in the media now can be believed. Only direct experience can be trusted and reported items considered as hearsay and viewed with a jaundiced eye. We welcome young journalism majors to join our ranks of opinion molders, reality benders and headline creators. Since there is no real news anymore, life through the media is a scripted reality show. Everyone used to enjoy watching Survivor on TV. Now y'all can watch the fake trials and tribulations of everyday America blasted across the tube or on the Interweb.

I would be remiss if I did not state my disdain for One America News Network

(OANN). Those bastards are actually trying to report what is really going on in the world. It is somewhat appalling having a contrarian view broadcast daily. I know instinctively that it is contrarian since it is not part of our scripted narrative.

On The Deep State

You've really got to hand it to these ass clowns. They've completely screwed the pooch. We had the federal government weaponized to the point where every federal agency was actively at war with everyone not in the Democrat Party. Try to think of any governmental agency that is not out to get the average, constitution loving American.

EPA – sue and settle while putting companies out of business. BLM – making ranchers sign agreements that they are not required to sign then chase them off their land for some bullshit compliance reason. Also, BLM is in charge of stealing all of the lands west of the original thirteen colonies for the federal government. IRS – conservatives need not apply for 501(c)3 status but we'll be happy to audit the shit out of you every year. Bureau of Indian Affairs (BIA) – suppressing Native Americans since 1608. How can an agency tell sovereign nations what they can and cannot do on their land? Government subsidies, that's how. Department of Education – can you say Common Core? You name the agency, I'll define our oppressive reaction.

Our coup de grace was the weaponization of the law and justice wings of the Executive Branch. How could they have been so sloppy and arrogant to expose the rot that existed through to their core? We had it made. We could level charges upon anyone or free anyone from any crime including treason. Nothing could touch us! We were the law!

All that is sadly drifting away. In the coming months, our minions will be fired, jailed or retire to fat pensions. It is a virtual circus available weekdays at 5, 6 and 11pm on your local conservative news channel. Luckily, there are not too many of those but just the same, our failings are ripped open for all to see. A painful reminder of what can happen when we believe we are truly invincible.

Think of all that had been achieved: Lerner and Koskinen get a pass; Daniel Love of the

BLM only gets fired; Loretta and Bill chat on the runway then Hillary is just deemed "careless"; Hildabeast again with the Benghazi debacle; those dipshits who ran Waco and Ruby Ridge walk scot free; the FBI establishes a kill zone and systematically executes a patriot rancher in the snows of Oregon; an illegal alien kills a woman in San Francisco and is exonerated; Holder with his Fast and Furious gun-running; and the Clintons sell one-quarter of our uranium stores in the Uranium One deal to the Russians without consequence.

An endless supply of amnesty for us and needless incarceration for our enemies. Our subterfuge became public all because two highly paid adulterous lovebirds could not stop texting one another. 50,000 texts; you've got to be kidding me. I've been married for over 30 years and don't think I've sent a thousand texts to my wife in that time.

Lest we forget, we injected spies into the Republican campaign so that we could entrap those who even dare speak with us. For the privilege of a short conversation, we'd turn your lives inside out unless you sing sweet songs of Russia, Russia, Russia into our ears. And I'd be remiss if I did not mention the dossier that our Democrat Party and Hillary's campaign paid to launch the fake investigation in the first place.

How could this have all come crashing down so quickly? It took years to embed all these operatives at the highest levels in our most sacred positions in government. Layer upon layer, we've weaved our minions within its highest ranks; progressive warriors bent on doing whatever it takes to make America part of the globalist utopia we have planned.

Thankfully, Mr. and Mrs. America have a very short attention span and even less of a willingness to do anything about it. To rise up and demand that heads role would require some admission of responsibility for letting these infidels root themselves in the seats of power where they act as judge, jury and executioner. When confronted with the true depths of what has transpired, they can only try to wish this away which is exactly why we'll get away with it once more. Which reminds me. How can we pin this on Republicans again?

On Representative Government part 2

Back in the time of the Founding Fathers, a government was devised with checks and balances so that no particular branch of the three grew to be too powerful. This system was predicated on the stipulation that as the Executive and Judicial branches of government grew, so did the watchers known as the Legislative branch that was comprised of citizen legislators.

Somewhere along the way, we figured out a way to hijack the system. Those of us who ascended to power in the Legislative branch coalesced our supremacy by limiting its membership. On the federal level, in 1911, our cohorts in Congress limited House membership to 435 without any nexus as to the genesis of that number. This completely obliterated Article 1, Section 2 of the Constitution that required a member of the House represent no more than 30,000 individuals. We did this without the benefit of a constitutional amendment thanks once again to Saint Woodrow Wilson. The same thing happened in California when its white supremacist 1879 Constitution restricted the number in the Assembly to 80 and the Senate to 40. Historically, both bodies had grown along with the population.

With the caps in place, our Executive and Judicial branches grew like wildfires with scorched earth policies such as Executive Orders, massive expansion of governmental agencies and legislating from the bench by the Judiciary. This was a direct result of limiting those who were to oversee the other two branches. As the watchers, we protected our power through incumbency and could care less that our oversight responsibilities had been abdicated. As long as we could guarantee our own re-elections, the people's interests were brushed aside.

This system continues to feed itself. Impotent legislatures create an exclusive club that limits membership for its own benefit. Other more qualified citizens need not apply. In turn, the Executive branch continues to grow beyond the bounds of its constitutional restrictions because the only group empowered to stop them is limited in both number and willingness to buck the status quo. The same can be said of the Judiciary as the Legislative branch has relinquished its law-making responsibility to the gang in black.

Now, "We the People" are truly in a quandary. The legislative branch is so small that the other two are left to grow unchecked. Fortunately, our Founders knew that government could not suppress its own insatiable appetite for power. They provided you with a remedy of last resort. Look it up; it's the 2nd on the list.

About the author

Mr. Baird is a sixth generation Californian from the gold mining days in the Sierra Foothills. He's a computer nerd who also loves history, politics and finance. A married father of two, he enjoys trying to right the wrongs of the world one mind at a time. But be warned, as an INTJ, he's hard to keep up with and even harder to slow down.

www.16personalities.com/intj-personality

www.mykvetch.com

Contact him at mykvetch@gmail.com

www.ingramcontent.com/pod-product-compliance
Lightning Source LLC
Chambersburg PA
CBHW072010040426
42447CB00009B/1576